LAUNCHING

LAUNCHING

Octavia Cyr

Border Press Books
PO Box 3124
Sewanee, Tennessee 37375

borderpressbooks.com
victoria@borderpressbooks.com

Copyright © 2020 Border Press Books

Border Press Books
PO Box 3124
Sewanee, Tennessee 37375
www.borderpressbooks.com
victoria@borderpressbooks.com

All rights reserved. No part of this book may be used in any manner without written permission

ISBN: 978-1-7346802-3-2

Library of Congress Control Number: 2020947289

Frostispiece image from *Pickerel Weed* glasswork by Karen Bourque.

Book design by Border Press Books
Printed in the United States

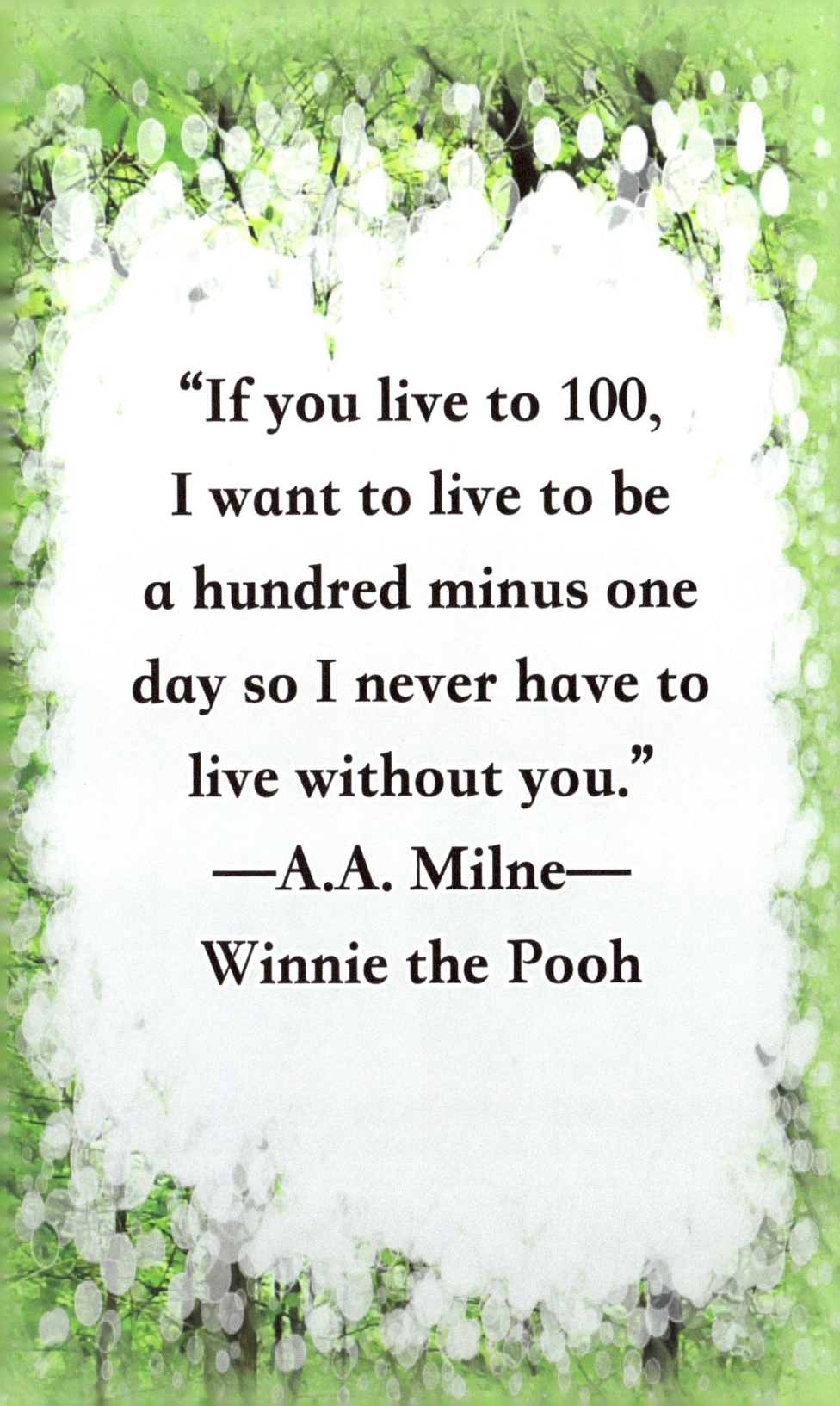

"If you live to 100, I want to live to be a hundred minus one day so I never have to live without you."
—A.A. Milne—
Winnie the Pooh

PART I

FOR THE ASKNG

Give me your mouth ... and I will drown in silence ... give me your mouth ... when I fail with words ... give me the eye of ... the eyes that fail on nothing ... and I will abuse their resistance.

DAISIES WILL TELL

You said, I was in my herbarium ... (and I don't know how to spell it) ... It means those plants ... unfolding, stretching ... stalktown ... and you in the center ... searching upward ... your face ... a knowing stem.

A GOODLY PORTION

In a book of adolescent memoirs ... a gold cover with a blue-eared demon ... beside someone smiling too hard ... because she is eighteen ... and irreverently wise ... the words hang their 25-year imprint: ... "I am a part of all that I have met" ... Ruefully, I paraphrase ... "and some are never met ... and if there is a feast in me ... You are free to all you partake.

TO YOUR HEALTH

If you run fast enough ... perhaps you will outrun ... the vagabond time which ... poor clown that he is ... thumbs his nose at you ... and me ... if you eat long enough ... the parent digestion ... will prove ... you have health enough ... to joust with time ... and, perhaps ... outlive the years ... that I will manage ... to steal from you ... despite so infrequent a feast.

LASTING ROMANCE

Let us attempt to hold ... the ghost of one love ... and let us not ... infract the whole.

FASTING

I fast because my child does not accept ... that best thing offered her ... offered me in too many years ... You ... I fast for conciliation ... You are puzzled ... become a conveyor ... a concerned tube of hourly juices ... thrusting them on me ... so I won't sway dizzily ... when I look into the better feast: your eyes ... In the night I dream ... my mother seeks me with terrible arms ... to pull me into her death ... and I cry ... You hold me in foster maternity ... murmur that no one will take me from you ... I try to believe you ... fasting, fastening ... on natal trust.

INFINITY OF GAZE

I liked you ... from the eyes up ... and the eyes down ...
from the rash beginning ... Always, I will like you ...
beginning ... and ending ... in your eyes.

MMMM

I've accused you of being spacey ... but your language actually murmurs ... who else would say: ... ears mumble ... women are *volumptuous* ... and coy eyes have eyegasms

WE LIVE TOGETHER

We live together ... talking of the social ... moral ... economic implications of living together ... The time, you say, is desultory ... talking about living together ... living, talking together ... The room is filled with cat fur ... dust ... a fan whirring ... books tumble from a shared bureau ... books about food ... running ... playwrights ... winning souls ... and that awful one on urine analysis ... to determine the disease ... you will die of ... (to bear out the author's thesis) ... I do most of the talking ... (maybe I'm the one who is living?) ... catch my breath ... while you shake your head hopelessly ... and laugh at the poem I wrote ... when we began to live together ... "In your silence I am too much conversation."

CAT PADS

Why, I ask you ... why the sleek black cat ... yours ... and the dizzy calico ... mine ... always curled in the bedroom ... in front of our fan? ... They sense love, you explain ... one, too old ... wanting to doze in retrospect ... the other, too young ... eager to develop feline technique ... Maybe ... But why can't they watch television?

ONE WAY STREET

Years ago, she warned me ... no one can stand that intensity ... I heeded her ... tried to wall out the illegal feeling ... But you opened me ... open me again and again ... as I turn, caressing your back ... in faltering darkness ... kissing your neck ... and thin lip ... sometimes cold on mine ... unknowing of such intensity ... You opened me ... and I can warn myself no longer ... Into the arms of loneliness ... I return ... with intensity ... feeling misguided.

BEING AND KNOWING

Being with you is as near as I come to being ... Being with you is as the first experience of quickening ... My two daughters nudging ribs in life joining ... Being with you is a climate ... where I go to lighten up ... so I don't have to travel far ... for the sun's perspective ... Being with you is a constant ... of time alive ... as if you are being ... just for me.

LAUNCHING

You once wrote about freedom ... "casting off, champagne glass in hand" ... and I drank in the scene ... trying so hard to keep your glass filled ... knowing four bottles had gone flat for you ... while drinking Dickinson's inebriate dew ... I wonder when you'll shatter glass ... against the bow again ... keeping only the label.

BEGGAR LOVE

Poets are obsessed with the poverty ... of other people's feelings, I said ... They try to create for others new feeling ... or recreate the old feelings ... others have misplaced ... They're also trying to lengthen the fleet ... of fleeting feelings, and ... Oh, stop, you cried ... Don't you ever get felt out ... Come here, I answered ... and feel me ... so I can adjudge the state of your poverty ... and your green eyes flooded mine ... with the message ... Indigent.

A NIGHT OF SLEEP

One bedtime story ... You turn me on ... then turn you over.

THE FINISH LINE

I couldn't write her kind of poem ... I didn't see the race your former lover saw ... To me, you had won it years ago ... the day you claimed ... your body important enough ... to be free, flesh free ... You run for me all the time ... your thin lip crossing the finish line ... of just my lip met and met again ... And I've run so far with you ... I tread sweat and salt just thinking ... how much of a race it has been ... Yet you, you eased into it ... with just one look ... as my heart, poised on the stem ... of your coveted stop-watch ... began, right then, to measure ... the miles and miles and miles ... and the many times ... you would win me ... I hope that doesn't make you a loser.

INVOLUTION

Love seems like a trap, you say ... and so you think of springing back ... to some independent safety ... The love that traps us all ... is love of Self ... and it holds the inherent danger.

FORBIDDEN FRUIT

I have taken upon my world ... to tell the world ... that love has flattered the marketplace ... dropped its casual fruit ... upon a rusty scale ... unbalancing the old rod ... with slow needle ... which cannot turn quickly enough ... to weigh in its gain ... love dropped from a laden tree ... whose roots go flaming through the earth ... whose roots go plotting the maiden soil ... branches inward branching ... incursive plunging ... narrowing the margin of safety ... flaunting the bird's trespass ... I have taken upon my world ... to trade the world ... in this marketplace of touch ... to taste the fruit ... whose forbidden skin ... pushes my flesh ... into the sword of choice ... and sweetens round the firm-grown pit ... I have taken upon my world ... the knowing tree ... whose roots go flaming through my heart ... whose branches go green ... in my searching mouth ... hallow my nodding desire ... that I may fall bidden, ripe ... into soft fields.

WIND SONG

Leaves skittering ... in the wind-broken dark ... like my ancient fears ... skittering before your hands ... fine in my hair.

ADORATION

I don't know what linnets are ... and animals gambol across my unconscious ... as if they knew the playground ... when it is really a private zoo ... I keep having dreams where I tell others ... you adore me ... and, yet awaken with folded arms ... in the strange, half-strained light of fall ... cushioned against a violent fray of weather ... the post of history, stoic limb ... mocks my safety ... threatens to give me away ... to the unsparing eye of my world ... creation, a map of desire ... the telltale bird, the angry sun ... a foolish wind from the back garden ... fans at life ... forces me outward ... so that sleep cannot get at me ... but I find someone listening at the door ... daring me to dare ... to dare to take ... what could be mine.

THE REFUSE OF MY LOVE

Today, our garbage can ... torn and crushed aluminum ... became red label condemned ... Prophecy? ... We broken eggshells ... scattered in the streets?

NIGHT OWL

The owls cry ... and baste their ohs ... with paralyzed dreams ... the owls cry ... rapt midnight ... to their get some prey ... in the large print of darkness ... in the bell of no-reason ... I sense their despair ... outlasting the moon ... outlasting the Gothic nest ... crying, let the go-so-round of my eyes ... and the go-so-claw of my need ... please peace ... in the tent of night.

YOU, OF INDEPENDENT HEALTH

Alone, I feel dark matter ... and feeling, remember your bright health ... languidly toast your runs ... sweat, clenched hands ... and wet curls on your high forehead ... I sleep cold ... artificial wind blowing ... keening on my unused body ... body being "one of the little answers ... to the larger questions of the soul" a marathon runner once wrote ... My hands fold ... across the disease of separateness ... knowing you laughing somewhere ... in long stretches of sand ... and family love ... and I wish you that small joy ... yet, am lonely for your smile ... my darling, your health.

SUMMER/WINTER

Before October the sky clears ... and all the salt days ... which have isolated our feelings leaf off ... Before fall, love is Dresden ... paper lace ... but soon it will bundle ... like the dream I had of you ... leaning over me in a ski hood ... I reached up and your cheek was warm ... Even come up from snow.

INVULNERABILITY

You say it is hard ... and we compare hardness ... as if grief had a degree ... a graph plowing certitude ... as if love ... made its own plateaus ... and climbed to prove ... that mountains best valleys ... and seas outlast land ... as if strength made merit ... only on hard being harder ... and hardness proved the inconstancy ... of all the inconstants ... the human heart ... It is hard ... but I am not harder ... and why should I be?

PART II

NIGHT BLOOMING

Night hands coax awake ... old blossoms, bursting flat seeds ... scattering in you.

FLOOD

All night the tortured dog ... tried vainly to chase his tail in the rain ... wailing, barking, twisted in the rusted chain ... At 3 a.m. In monsoon and no moon ... You, in slicker, boots and terrible anger ... led him out of the yard ... disguising your kindness as dognapping ... while I hugged you to the part of me ... which had hungered for mate tenderness ... nigh on 20 years ... Well, you said ... there's no doubt about it ... we'll have to move to another house ... tomorrow?

In your logic ... lies our protection.

BECAUSE TODAY I COULD NOT CHASE BUTTERFLIES

A tense reflexion of wind ... blows my butterfly away today ... I look for the ephemeral flute of wing ... listen for the little harp of your banter ... and, oh, I am frightened again ... by the short span of beautiful things ... I tried putting stones around the garden ... but they smothered the flowers ... and, why, then, would my butterfly visit?

THE WORD

While reading, I came across the word ... "Contiguous" ... It sounded close ... like wood fire in winter ... and I know we are ... that word.

IN EIGHT HOURS, YOU DON'T APPLY

Breakfast sometimes hits a long run ... one hour ... And yesterday you bathed at noon ... The summer winds down to weeks of ... trips to the public library ... awkward visits with friends and family ... running ... long walks ... movies ... now and then music ... shifting ideas bred in newly respectful love ... neither of us having been loved with respect ... as we shift papers and books ... from room to read ... to no room ... to read ... writing or talking of writing ... In languishing freedom and poverty ... you level me with the bemused query ... "Should I ask in my inquiry letter ... "By the way, do I work all day?"

LOVE FOOD

I never knew nutrition was a religion ... until you became the better part of my health ... soy ... groats ... carrots ... celery ... wheat berries ... a carnival of seed and plant ... On a melancholy day ... you made potato soup with yoghurt ... put more silver on the table than I could use ... And I found that if your religion ... would not resurrect ... it would restore.

ALTER AMBITION

You put aside "American Opinion" ... sprawl on the blue bedspread again ... agonizing over Ambition ... the capital pride ... Decide, in turn ... to become a carpenter ... to open a health food restaurant ... write a book on exotic fruits and vegetables ... to challenge Wall Street investors ... with your acumen for turning a dollar ... (like buying five acres of ... submerged swamp in Florida ... which you paid out in ten years) ... sigh, furrow ... ask me not to react so violently ... when I sob that I have robbed you of ... Ambition, the capital pride ... then utter: ... "Damn, your reaction makes me realize ... I can handle anything" ... You help me prepare a nine-page resume ... of my limited education and experience ... saying: a job may turn up for you anytime" ... and return to reading "American Opinion" ... (of your Ambition??).

INFORMAL EDUCATION

My expression ... is no profession ... but a lecture note ... your arms prepared ... your lips declared ... your devotion schooled ... the divine instruction ... comes through you ... professor of plants ... all green, growing me wise ... to my own nature.

STOPWATCH

Time is running out ... You must be pushing it along ... running those mean miles daily ... I can't clock mine ... the acceleration would frighten me ... I keep alive, like Sylvia Plath ... by right of poem ... and understand her more and more ... no money ... the threat of love ended ... In the storm she smiled ... all the while ... a lampshade smile for people dropping in ... who judged her "so self-contained" ... I know the judgment ... it excuses them all from having to care ... But she kept hoping ... with poet's grand intensity ... hoping someone would give her more time ... for Self (not so contained) ... for poems (not so smiling) ... Surely she realized it was a bad race.

TO LOVE WELL IS TO LOVE WELL

I know what it is…that restless thing ... that resistless burden ... prowling in my heart ... It is the wish to find some new way ... to write the feeling some can be betrayed by love ... that is not an art.

THE LAST CHANCE

I came in from some cornerstone of respectability meet ... feeling slightly respectable ... despite a small body of private opinion ... surrounding our clandestine love ... and found you tearing up your past ... letters notes, loves ... a weak smile on our face ... as if you were parting with secret ideals ... yet throwing me a kiss, saying ... I'm ready to settle in ... You have to be the last or I won't last ... I trust that moment ... even with you spinning miles away today ... and the room, the very wood so wooden ... opens ... opens wide ... the door banging behind our entry ... into the Last Chance Saloon.

WE HAVE GIVEN OUR HEARTS AWAY

You hold me in final caress ... so meek an assent ... to mood-altered Passion ... which, after all ... is wind sent ... wind spent ... Why, I cry ... why you ... why me ... Why have I not been given ... to give someone that final caress ... So meek an assent ... to mood-altered content.

DO YOU SEE THE SAME TRUTH?

The whole basis of love ... according to a mentor ... the late C. S. Lewis ... lies in a single question ... Do you see the same Truth? ... I spent hours trying to explain ... the essence of the Holy Spirit ... in a private religious revival ... staged in the big tent of our world ... a cramped bedroom ... asking, do you see the same Truth? ... You spend hours spinning records ... and let Robert Welch ... tell me about Creeping Communism ... in your private political rally ... staged for me to see the same Truth ... We spend months tracing the history of intellectual growth ... test out truths on one another's conscience ... and, together ... flunk the Science of feeling ... arriving at the same Truth ... Feelings can't be systematized.

PART III

VITAMIN STRENGTH

Did you actually read to me ... Divorces occur when a couple has serious calcium loss? ... Why do you mistrust the duration of our relationship? ... You take calcium daily.

RECIPROCITY

The law of feeling is return.

A RUDE AWAKENING

I am suspicious of Sleep ... part of your master plan for Health ... I once thought that people who lay abed ... wrinkling into stale sheets ... while others spread a lunch cloth ... were dangerously bored ... but you say you're not ... You often doze into a long kiss ... suffer three languid jerks ... and hum into a world filled with trees ... (because trees symbolize your hiding place ... from old feelings like Puritan Guilt and Mounting Fear ... because trees are old enough to be wise, you say) ... I envy the sleep ... resent bold yawns ... lie awake ... realizing that wakefulness can be ... dangerously boring.

"WHY MUST THE TEST OF ANYTHING BE ITS DURATION?"

My last love ... my last love" ... you say ... "You are different" ... My lost loves ... my lost loves, I think ... they were paper desire ... And when you turn from me ... in resistance of caress ... I lately wonder ... if your last love ... will last.

SAME-SAME

Every morning: eggs, any style ... brown bread and honey ... juice, tea, milk and bran ... "Don't you ever grow tired of same-same?" I ask ... (a saying my Persian houseboy taught me) ... You shift this slowly in cheek ... along with eggs, any style ... brown bread and honey ... lower that purdah shielding mysterious green eyes ... and throw the taut reply: ... "Don't you grow tired of same-same ... each night when we fare on love?" ... The answer is same-same ... No.

GOING AWAY

Baby, ... you get up ... and go away ... and I'm too old ... to catch up ... The sun today, pure memory ... rides to the bay ... where nets ... stretch over the sun ... glinting silver ... as my hair turning ... strands on your cheek ... on the boats rocking quiet ... there are no promises ... small chance of proving ... you're going to stay ... I'm going to stay awhile ... and then ... I'm too old to catch you ... but I'm riding to the bay again ... on pure memory ... your hands raising the sun for me ... and maybe it won't ... get up and go away.

WANDERLUSTS

Part of the summer we wandered in Mexico ... Seeds fell from the white summer sky ... and you, in league with health ... held an upturned hand, saying: "They are sun seeds ... eat them and you will be happy" ... I kissed the place ... where the sun had kissed your lonely freckles ... and ate the seed ... and grew happy ... We went home in the white summer sun ... the seeds with us ... but I fell ill ... as if they had become seeds of discontent ... You planted them shallow in that short time ... had no way of knowing ... that their wonder, small wonder ... had sprung from the wandering.

AMUSEMENTS

You lie beside me ... me, the former fascination ... a year or more again ... and you in a striped boy shirt ... reading about how urine analysis can determine your life expectancy ... I wish I were as boring ... Maybe I could amuse you by passing water ... Think how much deviation of disease I've disposed of ... to your lack of entertainment.

INNOCENCE HAS NO AGE

In the rain ... and your arms ... I felt your innocence ... incoherent only in sleep ... drowsing small noises ... in mime of Sue ... our adopted kitten ... who toyed with your coherent sleep ... In the rain ... scattering tin ... a downbeat making my heartbeat pound ... "Too rapidly," you said ... "for just lying there" ... I tried to tell you ... that your innocence ... the past barrier ... in some forgotten orange grove ... only tantalized ... keyed the heartbeat ... lengthened the vision ... of too many arms around you ... (yet too few caring holds) ... so that when I touched your lips in the rain ... and the new sleep of morning ... your mouth was young again ... and I was trusted to keep ... your innocence.

BATTLE LINES

You look as though you have known terror ... and relenting, kissed it to sleep ... What you have conquered in obduracy ... I have lost in constancy; ... You appear as one who has suffered too well ... and, I, too long ... Why do I feel a battle going on around us.

RUNNING AND BEING

Easily inspired ... you read aloud Sheehan's *Running and Being* ... part of the odyssey to Mexico ... You ran up and down ... unawed by the 4500 ft. mountain in Chipinque ... didn't develop a cramp ... I put on the new running shoes you had bought for me ... (because I survived a ten-minute run one day) ... walked a few steep gradients ... to view a dilapidated mountaintop zoo ... developed chest pains ... went to bed with my inspirations ... to ponder a thought ... projecting from your jutting chin ... then angry with anxiety ... the thought you wouldn't express ... you don't allow yourself ... anger and anxiety ... "I'll run ... You be."

GOALS

You tell me I must use time from you ... to do important things ... but when you part from me each morning ... face closed against my undoing ... I recognize the important thing ... is doing you.

WILL SET THE FLOWER FREE

And rain is the sound ... of earth wrinkling ... in love with desperation ... each drop in counterpoint ... rephrasing: ... to be alone ... to be alone ... the drone of time too long for justice ... the earth is merciless ... and the rain its whore ... to be alone ... to be alone ... washing in the words ... washing out the words ... the water goes down deep ... cautioning the parent of sleep ... isolation is merciless ... time pelts single globes ... which burst in the earth ... wrinkling in love with desperation ... Forgive my love ... forgive my love ... It has no choice ... only the art of wonder ... will push the flower through ... only the merciless earth ... and the rain down rain ... will set the flower free.

IN ANSWER TO SELF FLAGELLATION

You are ... as you always are ... not so deserving of self-crucifixion ... as you think ... as you keep searing your own flesh ... in has-been shadows ... you are simply ... inviolate.

OTHER PEOPLE'S DISAPPROVAL

Under pain of sentiment ... I am offered character.

BEING CHURCHED IN ONE ANOTHER

Once you said: "I am in awe of you" ... Me awesome? ... You make me tremble ... on the phony blue velvet bedspread ... someone else's seduction scenery ... you sit, one knee under you ... the way you sat when I fell in love with you ... I think about the maxim: ... "There are times when whatever be the attitude of the body ... the soul is on its knees" ... I shop for kneeling cushions.

UNDONE

The storm was hard laughter ... Yet, like summit lightning ... You passed through me ... Splitting the scar ... of a weather-piercing tree.

ANOTHER DOUBLE ENTENDRE

I haven't known enough happiness ... to make the identification ... I haven't known enough identity ... to create the happiness.

TO FLEE OR NOT TO FLEE

Your chin doesn't want to marry ... it'll never settle in ... And your eyes pose long voyages ... even if your arms haven't set sail ... When I am preoccupied with these features ... I don't know whether to propose or to take a long trip.

THE FALCON PAST

You say you don't know, it could end ... you've had too many bad experiences ... Little is known about experience ... It is faithless, trackless, heedless of terminals ... If you go back to slay the weeds ... a forest springs up ahead ... The problem lies in thinking ... it has made you grow ... taller than the forest ... or faster than the weeds? ... Little is known about experience, except that ... you cannot ignore its predictions.

MOURNING SONG

Do you know what the bird said? ... The one who sang as we made love? ... Do you know? ... He said you are my found tree ... But I, I have no nest.

THE STEM OF ECSTASY

Darling, how particular the flowers are ... blooming cold on the cover of a green book ... thrusting themselves at me ... the way you press your hip ... solely into my adjoining ... Darling, the flowers are ... startled poems ... scarlet lyrics ... pressing their earth philosophy ... on me, unsettled me ... Darling, our summer unspent love ... met today in a close attic ... where my tongue found your fulsome ... created, recreated lip ... Darling, thank you for the flowers ... and the look that tells me ... you are you and I am you ... That we are as much photosynthesis ... as the grand explanations in the book ... Darling, I need your flowers ... As I pick not-so-gently anymore ... the stem of ecstasy so hard.

THE BODY REPUBLIC

At 2 a.m., while discussing The Conspiracy ... and World Take Over (Communism) ... In the protectorate of your arms ... I felt life, liberty, and the pursuit of happiness ... wondered if you sensed ... my laissez faire.

MEXICAN BUTTERFLIES

Moving toward mesa ... temporary strophes of blue solidarity ... yellow butterflies taunt my options ... mariposas skimming in numbers ... a bright exodus ... coasting canyon to mesquite ... little abandoned flutter trips ... and as I sit too long, thinking ... too many weeks ahead ... their incaution chides me ... to remember the feel of your gentle hands ... stroking me like swift butterflies ... your mouth, one nectar of freedom ... opening and opening ... postponing return.

TREE TAPS

I cannot shake the branches ... of a tree whose leaves ... have fallen late ... Your roots go down ... into an old forest ... where I am weary of wandering ... and each time I neglect to water you ... you pull up root.

SACRIFICE

If I had to live twice over again ... by threat or denial of you ... I would choose to live beneath threat with you ... as only ground leaf lives in shadow ... yet free in a new sun ... If I had to breakfast on fear ... and sleep leaning into barter ... I would lick the heels of terror ... rather than martyr you ... to such low gods of respectability ... You will never believe ... that I have moved on dare ... to dare myself ... into the claim of your proud love ... but I have ... and if I have ... can you outlast the threat?

FOREST LEAVES

When you put on tramping clothes ... and follow ransomed trails ... in search of plants I don't trust ... because I don't know them ... as you haven't made them known to me ... I feel improbable ... outside your time and space ... And I write minutiae ... while needing you gargantuan ... I think of lying on the bed of forest leaves ... dry and crackling under your spine ... the bright tilt of your eyes ... unsettling mine ... I am, my beloved ... I am only your mouth ... altering me.

WINGS

When you ... atmospheric free ... deep into my bleak eyes see ... a threat of unpredictability ... your wings, antimony flutters ... will pale ... all precious, unuttered ... fail.

MARTYR

Yeats said: "Too long a sacrifice ... can make a stone of the heart ... O when may it suffice?" ... Stones do not suffice ... nor blood ... nor crosses on the hill ... nor even the closed doors of single will.

FOREST IN THE NIGHT

Fie the mad moon of silence ... fie the rivulets making tracks ... where mad humans have never crossed ... the silence of mad moons ... in silence we drown as ... forests limping in the forsaken dark ... in silence we make woods ... to hold the light.

MISSING ME ONE PLACE, SEARCH ANOTHER

I miss you ... and have stopped at all the places ... I used to find you waiting ... as Whitman enjoined ... But you have gone ... not even pausing for a second's sentiment ... sharp like my mother's death ... I miss you ... and my former expectations.

QUICK SALE

Well, down to $17 and the end of ...
Summer Romance ... Better nomenclature:
... Penny Romance ... Did you get
your money's worth? ... Read on.

ABOUT THE AUTHOR

Octavia Cyr is a pseudonym for a poet who wishes to remain anonymous.

www.ingramcontent.com/pod-product-compliance
Lightning Source LLC
Chambersburg PA
CBHW040455240426
43663CB00033B/11